INTENTIONAL DECEPTION

BY

DELORES LYNCH COLEMAN

My Father's Mansion Press

Nashville Tennessee

Intentional Deception

ISBN-13: 978-0-9913127-3-3

Copyright © 2016

by **Delores Lynch Coleman**

My Father's Mansion Press

PO Box 78605

Nashville TN 37207

Lightning Source Inc.

1246 Heil Quaker Rd.

La Vergne, TN 37086

Dedication

I would like to dedicate this book to my loving mother, Letha: "You taught me everything except how to live without you".

To My husband, children, and grandchildren: You gave me the inspiration to complete this project and helped me to endure through all the pain with love and laughter.

To My baby sister Nicole: You are an amazing woman who loves everyone and will give your last to help someone in need. I am truly blessed to have a sister who has been by my side no matter what!!

To My cousin and best friend forever, Curtis Williams: Words cannot express how much you influenced my life for the better, and how much I miss you!!

Tto My brothers, Donald, Maurice and Tyrone: I am grateful to you for protecting me since we were kids and helping me with my children whenever I asked with no complaints. I love you all unconditionally!!!

Acknowledgement

I want to acknowledge and thank all the powerful women who have supported me through my journey from a young child to becoming the woman I am today. Viola Floyd, Beverly Bowens, Aline Sims, Jenice Dunlap, Gloria Pringle, Sharon Pettus, Jeanie Vines and Cora Benson

My Sister Friends who have been by my side through the good times and the storms and I truly cherish each and every one of you for being a gift in my life. Kim Wise, Deidre Anderson, Melanie Saffold, Angela Everett, Lavern Walls-Bacon, Patricia Jolly, Audrey Nuby and Joy Hines Ross

A special thanks to Rita Brown for introducing me to Mrs. Diana Tittle who helped me learn the art of becoming a serious writer and believing that I could accomplish this dream.

I want to say how grateful I am to Mr. and Mrs. Mike Marshall for your continued support of my family throughout the storm, but we prevailed because of the love you unselfishly gave to us all.

I am forever grateful to my cousin, Rev. Barbara A. Woods, for all your hard work with editing and publishing this book. I couldn't have done this without you!!! Thank you very much!!!

Introduction

You never know how life is going to take you for a spin. Here I am a grown woman, married with children and successful in a good career when all of a sudden my maternal grandmother surprises me with the truth about what really happened to my mother. We sat down for a while and she revealed to me the reason my mother was involved in the Federal Witness Protection Program and the lifestyle that she lived in the drug business.

I was devastated and shocked to hear this unbelievable news, but I was relieved that my grandmother Lottie was finally ready to talk to me about the burden she carried around for so many years and how she supported my mother's decision. Now, it began to make sense to me of the difficult childhood that I had to deal with growing up in separate households and having to move around constantly without a solid and stable family foundation.

My mother was violently murdered when I was 16 years old and I could never understand why someone would shoot a mother of six children eight times. I was curious to know and I needed to find out why.

My grandmother told me that a friend of hers was in the county jail, and during that time her friend met a woman by the name of Debbie, who was also in the county jail on the same floor as this friend. Anyway, it was a coincidence that Debbie just happened to be my mother's best friend and she was present when my mother was murdered. Learning all of this made me eager to find out all that I could pertaining to my mother's life and death, so I have spent over 20 years piecing this story together.

My determination stems from my desire to help other young people who find themselves involved in the drug scene or any other difficult situation and help them to realize that there is a way out. I don't want to see another young woman murdered or another young man sent to prison for the rest of his life because they are seduced into the same kind of lifestyle.

I decided to do some investigating on my own, so I started asking my close relatives what they knew about the whole ordeal involving my mother. I took that information to start and I even went further by going to the FBI to see if I could get the records of the proceedings involving the case, but I was told that the records were sealed indefinitely, which probably means forever. I was upset of course, but I did not let that stop my determination to get this story told, and even though it has been many years since I lost my mother, the memory of her gives me the motivation to tell others why they don't want to choose the wrong path in life.

Chapter One
Happy Childhood

Growing up in Cleveland can be challenging at times, but you learn to adjust to your environment the best way that you can. My parents were both 19 years old by the time that I was born on a hot summer day in July the 3rd of their Six children. I could not have asked for better parents because they seemed to love each other very much and I was very happy as a child to feel the love they showed me every day.

I remember happier times so vividly and how we spent time together going to the park and out to dinner to eat and sometimes we might even get a chance to go see a good movie at the theatre downtown which was so exciting. I cherish all those memories so much because my life seemed to change so drastically overnight.

I reflect back to the day when the police came to our house looking for my father, but he did not want to talk with them so he climbed out of a window in the back of our house and proceeded to run through the backyard and jump over a fence. When the police noticed that he was running they ran after him, but they did not catch him that day.

I was about nine years old when all this happened and I felt very confused and did not understand why the police would be chasing after my loving father. My mother never explained anything to us at all about what just occurred, but she did send us to our bedrooms wondering what all this confusion was about. I was angry that no one wanted to talk to us about why the police wanted to take our father away from us because he was everything to me and I was his little princess and he gave me everything that I ever wanted and I could never see him doing anything wrong.

He never came back home that day and my mother told us that he would be away for a while and I was deeply hurt by this news, but during this time was when I learned about prison and why people had to go there and be away from their families. It was all too much for me to handle at that age because my father always took good care of his family and we loved each other very much. It was not going to be easy for me because every little girl needs her father around to protect her. So, when our house caught on fire about a year after my father's absence, it was devastating for my family because we lost everything and there was no insurance policy on our house.

The firemen rescued my eldest brother Donnie from a second floor bedroom window while we all stood outside screaming for him to jump because the flames were blazing everywhere. I knew that he had to be scared because I was scared myself. Donnie escaped with minor cuts and bruises and he was going to be just fine, but most of all we were grateful for his life and that we were all safe. Unfortunately, we had no place to live, but the Salvation Army helped us for a few weeks until my mother found us suitable housing.

Well, to our surprise we were now going to be residents in a low income housing development which was known as "the projects". I had never lived in the projects before, but I had a great Auntie whom we called Mama Kay and she had lived in the projects for years. We would always have a good time visiting her because

2

she would buy all the latest songs that were popular back then and she loved to watch us do the latest dances that were popular on the radio. I really enjoyed spending time with her, but I did not like roaches and she had them bad, so I never wanted to eat anything at her house when we would visit her.

I was a little girl growing up in the inner city ghetto and I never thought about what my life would be like in ten, twenty, or even thirty years. All I cared about was having fun outside, eating good food, and playing outside with all my best friends.

My parents had been separated for nearly three years when my father did time in prison and during that time my mother entered into a drug rehabilitation center to help with her addiction to heroin. While she was there she met a man who would later become her companion and the reason why her life would never be the same. I will call him Butter because he was a yellow man and his demeanor was very unlikable to me.

My mother started living with him shortly after our first house caught on fire and during the time my grandmother was caring for us. I learned later that my mother was paying my grandmother money to take care of her kids while she formed a relationship with Butter.

My grandmother Lottie was very strict and she had us trained like soldiers in an army and we were to never do anything without her permission. We had no choice but to obey all her rules at all times or else there would be consequences to deal with, and you did not want to make her angry. She did not tolerate lying or stealing and we better not ever think of talking back to her. Honestly, I was very afraid of her because she was a strong and loud woman and would scream at you if you did something wrong or not the way she expected it to be done. Back then I thought she was the meanest person on the earth, but I realize now that she was preparing us for the tough world that we had to grow up in. She knew that life was not going to be easy for any of us and I will always be grateful to her for having our best interest at heart.

My father was eventually released from prison after three years and I was very happy when he told my grandmother that she would be free from her duties of caring for his children. Now that he was home, he would be responsible for taking care of us, so she had no choice but to respect his decision. I know my father appreciated all the hard work my grandmother had put in caring for us, but he did not want his children living in the projects, so he moved us out right away and my grandmother moved into an apartment by herself. He moved us from the projects into a small three bedroom house that looked so creepy from the outside and I did not even want to go near that house let alone sleep there.

When my father gave us chores to do, we did them with no problem. So, it was no surprise when he told us that we would be cleaning our new residence from top to bottom. It wasn't all that bad once we finished and moved our furniture in and got organized because we were going to be there for a while.

We had lived at this house for about one year and then it was time for Len, who is my second oldest brother, and I to graduate from elementary school. I was voted by my class to give the sixth grade graduation speech and I was very excited about that. I don't know why my father did not attend our graduation, but my mother and grandmother was there to see us accept our certificates and be promoted to junior high school.

After our graduation my father moved us to another house which was larger and had more space for us to move around in. We even had a large backyard and a basketball hoop that he attached above the garage so we could play outside during the nice weather. Life was wonderful for me and I had a new best friend named Ivy, and she was only one year older than I was. Ivy had four sisters and one brother and they lived just a few houses away from ours. Her single mother was very beautiful and she dressed really nice and would always smile whenever I went over to play with Ivy.

Their house was even larger than ours and they always kept it clean and tidy because their mother was strict and she wanted everything done before she got home from work and they never let her down. We had so much fun during the summer of 1976, but the fun had to end. The time was near for us to prepare for our return to school in September which was usually right after Labor Day.

But, something I never expected happened suddenly and the world around me changed forever. I remember falling asleep in my bed on a breezy fall night and the temperature was cool outside. The entire house seemed quiet and all the children were asleep because we had school the next morning. My mother and father were down in the living room talking when I went upstairs to go to bed for the evening. I was in a deep sleep warm and comfortable when suddenly my mother was screaming at me to wake up because the house was on fire.

The words did not register in my brain right away, but I listened and did what she told me and quickly put on my slippers and began to follow her down the stairs in my pajamas. I panicked and stopped before we could get to the first floor and told my mother that Nikki was still asleep in her bed, so we turned around and went back to get her. She was only five years old and very small, but my mother picked her up and we ran back down the stairs as fast as we could.

5

As we ran back down the stairs I was captured by the fire and the different vibrant colors of the flames, and even though it was breathtaking I was terrified of what would have happened had we not went back to rescue the baby, my only sister.

We all stood outside trembling and I knew the fire trucks were near because I could hear their sirens from a distance. When they arrived they put the fire out in time and the good news was that the entire house was not destroyed only the front porch because that is where the fire had started. We were grateful to a couple who had just left a nearby bar that night and while they were walking home they noticed the fire under our porch and ran up the steps to the front door and started banging until someone opened the door.

I'm not sure which one of my parents opened the door that night, but I am very thankful to that couple because had they not been there at that pivotal moment there is a chance that I might not have been here today to tell this story. Barely escaping that night was terrifying for me and my siblings. We were taken to the Salvation Army that night so that we would have some where to sleep. How could this happen to our family for a second time within a few years? Unfortunately, our family was experiencing another tragedy.

My mother stayed with us while we were at the Salvation Army for a few days, but when we returned to our house the smell of fire was still present and even though we did not lose any of our clothes they still had a burnt odor. There was not much structural damage to the house, but the front porch needed repairing. My father had someone to come and start the repairs and life went on as usual and we went to school for another few weeks.

Until one night around the middle of October my siblings and I were awakened from our beds by our parents and told to put some clothes on, so we did what we were told. As we left out the door we noticed a big van in our driveway and there were a few men outside waiting for us, so we all climbed in as well as our mother. This was very strange I thought to myself, but I was so sleepy and tired that I went back to sleep right there in my seat. When the van finally stopped and we got out the van, the two men that drove the van escorted us into a small motel room and we were told to make ourselves comfortable while they talked with my mother. We just stared at each other in amazement because we did not understand what was going on.

My oldest brother, Donnie was always the first one to offer his opinion and said that we were probably going on a vacation. That just did not make any sense to me when we had just begun a new school year. The year was 1976 and I was 12 years old in the 7th grade in junior high school. I knew I was maturing and I was so excited to be a preteen and venture into a new school year. Things were not going as I expected it to go and to my surprise we were in for a rude awakening.

A little while later my mother joined us in the room and we wanted to know what was going on and why all of us were here at this strange motel. She told us that we were going to be leaving Ohio and she was going to get a really good job so that she could take better care of us. I was puzzled because I already felt like we were being taken care of pretty well by my father and I never wanted for anything. My father always provided everything we needed as his children while we were with him, so I never felt like I missed out on anything as a child.

I knew our parents loved us very much, but I did not understand why all of this was happening to my family and I began to feel very sad and confused. My mother told us that my father would not be moving out of town with us. I never expected to hear those words and I was not happy anymore, but angry that the only man that I trusted would not be leaving Ohio with us. I knew that my father had served time in prison, but back then it was not explained to us that a felon could not leave the state of Ohio if he was on probation. As a kid I just wanted to be with both my parents, but that never happened again.

Before we left town my father was allowed to come and visit us at the motel for a little while, but we had to prepare ourselves to say goodbye to him with tears and tight hugs. We had no idea when we would see him again and it was very difficult to see him walk out that door and not come back. I will never forget that day because I felt abandoned and lonely without my father.

We stayed at the motel for a few more days and then one morning we were escorted back to the van, but this time we arrived at the airport. We were going to start a new life somewhere else, but the funny thing was, we did not know where we were going.

Chapter Two
Wisconsin Days

It was pure excitement to me riding on that plane that took off so fast before ascending into the air. The last time that I was on a plane was with my grandmother Lottie when I was a very small child and she had taken me to New York City where she lived most of her adult life. She was so happy that she had her first granddaughter to spoil, but my father had to put his foot down because she wanted me to stay there and live with her and he was not having that at all.

When the plane finally landed I was very eager to know where we were, so I started looking all around the airport for any signs that would help me, but I saw none. Once again there were a few men waiting at the airport to escort us to our next destination, but this time one of the men was a big black guy and he was very nice to us. There was another van waiting outside the airport for us and we all got in. Once we started riding, I noticed a sign with the words "Wisconsin". I assumed this is where we would be living because my mother never told us where we were going, but maybe she did not know either.

We arrived at a very nice hotel which was much nicer than the small hotel they had us at before we left Ohio. It even had a large swimming pool and a restaurant where we could eat some really good food. It really did feel like a luxurious vacation that we had never been on before. We were having the time of our lives, and after a while school did not seem important anymore.

We ate anything that we wanted and stayed up as long as we wanted to. We even made new friends with a family who were staying at the hotel while their dream house was being built and this was the very first time in my life that I had any interaction with someone of another race. I grew up with other black children, but I never had a conversation with someone my age that was not black. It was something new to me and at that time I never experienced any kind of racism because people were people to me and it did not matter if they were white. The only difference to me was the way they talked which seemed so proper to me.

We lived at the hotel for weeks, until our new home was ready. We finally moved into a town house with four bedrooms and two bathrooms, a large kitchen with a nice dining area and the living room was very spacious for all of us. I absolutely loved our new home and we were all ready to start our new school the next day. I could hardly sleep through the night because I was anxious to meet new friends and start a new learning experience.

The next morning my two older brothers and I were escorted into John Muir one of the largest schools I had ever seen in my life. We were at the age where we were attending junior high school, and my three younger siblings were in grade school. I remember being intimidated by my new surroundings because I had never seen so many different races of people in my life, but it was an exciting experience for all of us. I adjusted very well at our new school and learning new things was a challenge for me.

I made new friends, but it was all overwhelming at first because here I am a black girl from the ghetto in this strange place and I could not understand how I ended up here out of all the places we could have been in the world. All I knew is that I did not ask to be there, but I was going to make the best out of the situation I was given. It was a real culture shock for all of us because we had no black friends that we could relate to.

We made friends with our neighbors who just happened to be white during that time, which was no big deal to us as long as they treated us like they wanted to be treated. We lived right next door to an entire family just like ours and their mother was raising her kids by herself as well. The only difference between her and my mother is that her children disrespected her and talked back and called her derogatory names which surprised me and I even told them that they should never treat their mother in such a disrespectful way.

I told my mother about her and they had a chance to talk with one another. My mother was so kind and thoughtful to everyone that she came in contact with. She even gave our neighbor some furniture because she had none at that time. I noticed that our neighbor stayed in her home all day and smoked cigarettes constantly. I remember her being so sad all the time and she seemed so lonely even though she had many children.

We were all doing just fine until one afternoon the unexpected happened. Donnie, Len and myself were walking home from the store and two teenage boys started calling us derogatory names from their porch and telling us that we did not belong in their neighborhood. I just ignored them and I kept walking towards our house, but my brothers called their bluff and wanted them to come off their porch.

I don't know why those two white boys came off their porch that day, but they did. The next thing I knew they were all fighting each other and I could do nothing to break them up, so I ran as fast as I could back to my house and told my mother what was happening.

My mother and I ran back to the house and they were still fighting. My mother grabbed my brother Len off one of the boys, and then the same boy got up off the ground and ran over to his porch and came back with a big heavy chain. He went towards my mother swinging the chain at her, but Len intercepted and took the chain away from the boy. The next thing I knew Len had the boy on the ground and had wrapped the chain around the boy's neck and would not let go. The boy started choking and turning blue and my mother and I started screaming at Len so that he would let go of the chain, but he wouldn't. Donnie had to run over and use all his strength to grab Len off the boy or something worse could have happened like someone ending up in the hospital.

After that frightening altercation we all walked home and I don't believe that an entire hour had passed when suddenly there was heavy pounding at our door. My mother looked out the window and it just happened to be the father of the boys my brothers were fighting. He was furious and angry and started yelling outside of our door that he wanted the boys that were fighting with his sons to come outside. I was so afraid for them, but my brothers wanted to go out there and deal with their father too. My brothers were some tough boys who welcomed a fight and I never saw them back down from one.

My mother told us to go and sit down and stay away from the windows and the door and just be quiet. She told that angry man to leave from in front of her door because she was going to call the police, and he told her that he was the police. She had a look of disgust on her face, but she remained calm and walked over to the phone and made a call. I don't remember what she had said or who she said it to, but it had to have been very important because that angry man eventually left our door and the tension eased up a little bit.

We ate dinner and went to bed for the night, but I kept thinking about everything that happened that day until I fell asleep. We attended school the very next morning like we usually do, and rode the school bus home. The closer we got to the house we noticed a very big truck in front of our house. I wondered why a truck like that would be there, and as we walked through the front door I was in disbelief because our entire house was empty and I was devastated. I asked my mother what was going on and why was all of our furniture packed up on that truck outside. She told me that the altercation that happened yesterday caused some serious problems for my brothers and she was told that it would be best if she moved her family out of that neighborhood.

I was very young, but angry that we had to move again when we were just getting settled in our new home and schools. As we rode away I looked back to our house and I knew that I would never see that house again. The same men who transported us to Milwaukee were the same men who would escort us to our next destination which I had no idea where that would be. As we boarded the plane, I wondered where they would be taking us next. I just sat in my seat quietly and waited in anticipation until the plane took off again. We were on the plane for a couple of hours, but we never did this much traveling before and it just did not seem normal to me. When the plane landed at the airport we looked out the window and there was nothing out there that looked familiar to us at all.

Chapter Three
Here We Come Kansas City

When we arrived at the airport, there were two different men who would transport us by van to another hotel where we stayed for a few weeks until they found us a decent home to live in. We were in Kansas City and I had never heard of Kansas before besides on the Wizard of Oz movie growing up.

We spent a lot of time at the swimming pool in the hotel and we never got bored because we entertained each other. My mother never wanted to go swimming with us no matter how many times we would ask her. She would just stay in the hotel room all day and watch television and smoke cigarettes and she seemed to be so lonely at times. I would tell her how much I loved her and she would always tell me she loved me too, but I noticed that my mother would not eat much food and she was losing a lot of weight. Sometimes, she would have us go down to the hotel restaurant and order her some food and bring it back to the room.

There was one occasion when we brought her some food and she was not happy about how they prepared it. She told us to take the food back down to the restaurant because it was cold and not done and we did exactly what she told us to do. However, one of the cashiers told us that there was nothing that could be done about the food, so we went back to the room and told my mother what she said.

My mother got up and put on her shoes and stormed out of that hotel room so fast and we all got on the elevator with her and I could tell that she was very upset. My mother walked up to the cashier, who turned us away, and asked her why she did not take the food back and have the cook prepare it properly. The cashier told my mother that once the food leaves the restaurant there is nothing that they can do. The next thing I knew, my mother opened the container of food and shoved it right in her face and told her to eat it. Looking back, I know that poor cashier felt helpless, but my mother did not play around with people when she was serious about something. After that, we all walked calmly back to the room and she told us that we would be leaving that prejudice hotel very soon, and within a few days that is exactly what happened.

We were so excited about moving into our new town house with three floors. The arrangement was nice for all of us. My older brothers Donnie and Len wanted their own rooms because they wanted their privacy. My younger brothers Ty and Jay always roomed together and my baby sister Nikki and I shared a room, and my mother had her own bedroom. The kitchen was small so we ate in the dining area, but the living room was very spacious and my mother enjoyed inviting her friends over for parties. I did not like the smoking and drinking that was going on, but I was a child so I had no voice to say anything about what grown folks did.

My mother was working at General Motors soon after we moved in, so that left Donnie and I to prepare all the food for the family which I loved to do anyway. Donnie and I would take a cab to the supermarket and buy all the food that we liked eating and then take a cab back home and start cooking dinner. My mother worked second shift so we managed on our own. My younger siblings did not like to clean up, but I made sure they helped out because they were not going to leave me doing everything by myself, so I had to be tough on them.

We were the typical kids, but we would get into fights with each other all the time. I remember my older brothers fighting and knocked over a huge speaker on my little sister Nikki's foot and it was broken because of their fight and this happened when she was only five years old. My mother was very angry about this because it did not make sense for them to fight each other like they were enemies when they were brothers and should love one another. For some reason Donnie wanted to rule over Len, maybe because he was jealous of the relationship that my mother had with Len and how close they were. I knew how close my mother and Len was, but it never bothered me because I was very close to her as well. She was like my big sister and she knew that she could depend on me for whatever she needed help with and I would be there to support her no matter what was going on.

Our father never wanted us to know that he adopted my brother Donnie because he did not want him to be treated any different from the rest of us and he was loved and disciplined just like the rest of us. My father never showed any favoritism in our household when we were growing up. I would get so annoyed when our friends would ask us questions concerning the color of Donnie's skin and why he was so much darker than the rest of us. Well, at that time I never knew why, but I felt very offended because his DNA was not a factor to my parents, so why should anyone else care. I guess people would be curious because his features were a little different from the rest of his siblings.

It was difficult at times to remember not to tell my friends that our names had been changed when we moved to Kansas. I did not talk much about why we moved there in the first place. I just kept myself busy by participating in different activities at school. I even had taken an interest in gymnastics, but I had to quit because the gym was just too far away from where we lived and my mother had to work and did not have the time to transport me back and forth across town.

My favorite hobby was reading books and magazines. I would save my lunch money to buy the *Right On* magazine every month because they would have pictures of my favorite dancers and singers. I loved the way the women's hair would be styled, so I had very good examples of who I wanted to look and dress like. I was reaching puberty around that time and I started to develop into a teenager.

I no longer wanted to look like a boy, so I started taking my appearance a little more serious now that I was getting attention from boys at school. I had always played with boys because I had so many brothers of my own, but I never liked any of them in a romantic way. Until one morning as I was walking to one of my classes during my 7th grade year at school, I saw the most intriguing person that I had ever seen in my life. He was a boy whose name I did not know and a face that I would never forget.

He smiled at me and I felt butterflies all over my body, but I just kept walking because I was nervous and surprised that he even recognized me. Well, he did recognize me and he surprised me even more when he came to my house to visit, but I never told him where I lived. My brothers were very protective and they did not like when boys came around their sisters. I was very flattered and excited, but it took me a while before I would go outside to talk to him because I did not know what I was going to say. Eventually, I went on outside and he was sitting on his bike with this incredible smile. When I walked up to him, he told me his name was PJ and I told him my name. We talked for a little while until it got dark and I gave him my phone number so that he could call me. I did not want him coming back to my house so that my brothers could tease me even more than they did that day.

I never had a boyfriend before and I wanted PJ to be my first. We would talk for hours and hours on the phone into the late hours of the night until we both fell asleep. He was very kind and I felt like he really cared about me because he never asked me to do anything that made me uncomfortable. We would exchange pictures with each other and meet at the skating rink, but we never let anyone know how close we had really become. PJ was intelligent and a very good student at school. He had two brothers and they were raised by their hard working single mother.

He invited me to visit him at his home one day, but his mother was not there and I never told my mother that I would be going to his house. I told her that I would be at my best friend Lisa's house and that was true. They lived in the same housing unit which made it easier for me to visit both of them. I knew that I was very young and did not know much about love, but I felt very close to PJ and I would think about him all day every day until we would see each other again. He was my boyfriend now, so when we had our first kiss it was very romantic and I was infatuated to the point that all I wanted to do was be with him. By the beginning of 8th grade we were bussed to another school across town during the desegregation laws. It was such an inconvenience because we had to ride the school bus for over

30 minutes just to get to our school which made me upset, but I was always better when I saw PJ at school.

After a few months my mother decided to move us to another house which meant that we had to transfer to another school and I was devastated because I would no longer see PJ every day. I felt like my world was falling apart and I became withdrawn and unsure of how I would make new friends all over again. I did not like the house we moved into because it was old and much smaller. We adjusted to the new neighborhood and began to meet new friends.

My brother Len and I transferred to Northwest Junior High School and it was huge, but we were together so I felt safe. I joined the school choir because I loved to sing and I also became a cheerleader while maintaining very good grades. I worked hard at school and I knew that I could excel at anything that I put my mind to. There were times when I would occasionally have problems with other girls at my school. They did not like the way I dressed or how much confidence I had in myself, or the attention that I would get from other boys. It did not make things much better for me, so I had to fight and gain the respect that I deserved because I was not going to let anyone intimidate me or stand in the way of my education.

My mother taught me to always stand up for myself and never let anyone take advantage of me just to be their friend. She did not allow me to share clothes with friends because she knew that was the worst way to end a friendship. My mother always gave me the best advice and it has helped me to become the woman I am today. I admired my mother for her sense of style and how beautiful she was when she got all dressed up to go out with her friends. I would watch while she applied her makeup and she had a variety of wigs that she would wear. She could have been a movie star and she was such a lovely lady.

The end of the school year was approaching fast, so I had an opportunity to work as an usher for a small company who provided services for concerts, college and professional basketball games, and even the circus. This was my very first job and it was one that I really enjoyed because I met so many interesting people who came from all over the world. After working there for a few months, I asked my boss, Mr. Porter, if he would give my brother Donnie a job. He did, but Donnie did not work there long because he was dishonest. Donnie was always getting into some kind of trouble and kept my mother worried all the time. When he was 16 years old he was arrested for stealing a cab because he wanted to go joy riding with a friend and I'm sure it was exciting until he drove into a ditch. It never made any sense to me why Donnie chose to do the things he did, but when he wanted something he always managed to get it.

There was a time when I was too embarrassed to let a friend of mine know that Donnie had taken her mother's car one winter morning when she started the car to warm it up and then went back inside the house. Donnie just took off in her car and did not think anything about it. I don't know where they found the car, but the police did find it. When my friend told me what happened I acted surprised like it was the first time that I even heard about it. I had to keep secrets about a lot of things that was going on in my family and I did not like doing that, but you have to protect those that you love the best way you know how.

My grandmother Lottie was married by the age of 16 to a very abusive husband who treated her disrespectfully and was not supportive of his own daughter, who was my mother. She eventually left him and moved to New York City, but left my mother in Ohio to be raised by her mother and she never wanted any more children after my mother was born.

Lottie came to visit us at our home one summer while we were still living in Kansas City. She told me all about her life with that man and it made me very sad that she had to endure that type of abuse, so she left him because she wanted a better life for herself and her daughter. My mother and Lottie were both very strong women and sometimes they would disagree on certain matters and I would hear them arguing all the time and there seemed to be a lot of resentment.

There was a time when my older brothers were being disrespectful and started talking back to Lottie, which made her angry. She went in her purse and pulled out her gun on them, which scared them. They ran up the stairs to their bedroom and locked the door just to get away from her, but they never disrespected her again. I don't think that she would have actually shot them, but she did not play with anybody. Lottie had told me that she shot her abusive husband because he kept harassing her even though she had a restraining order against him. I don't think he ever bothered her again after that happened.

My mother was very upset about what happened and she told Lottie that she could not treat her boys in that manner. Lottie's feelings were deeply hurt by what my mother said to her. So, she left out the house angry and sat in her car with her gun and locked all the doors and started crying for hours until my mother pleaded with her to come back in the house and work things out. Lottie was a very emotional woman because of all that she had experienced in her life and I understood why she felt that way as I grew older. I was very happy that everything worked out fine that day for all of us because I did not want anyone to get hurt.

My Grandmother Lottie had back surgery while she was visiting us in Kansas City. When it was time for her to return home, my mother allowed her to take Ty, Jay, and Nikki back with her to Ohio because she needed help and raising 6 children was really hard for her. I was very sad to see them leave, but I knew that Lottie would take very good care of them

I was entering 9th grade and I looked forward to my last year of junior high school so I continued to make good grades and I even participated in the school beauty pageant and I won a first runner up trophy and a beautiful crown. I was very proud, but I really wanted my mother to be there for me and I know she would have if she did not have to work that day. I received a lot of attention after the pageant and there were quite a few boys that wanted to be more than just a friend. I knew that they were after one thing and that was my virginity. I kept my distance because I was not going to let anyone take advantage of me. My relationship with PJ was innocent and he was very respectful of me and I really appreciated that quality in him because most of the boys I knew were not like that.

I had to learn at an early age how to avoid getting involved with anyone that did not have my best interest in mind. I had so many good memories during my 9th grade year, but it was time to start planning to attend the prom and I had not been asked by any of my classmates at school. I was very happy when PJ asked me if he could take me to my prom and I eagerly accepted. I did not expect PJ to take me since he attended another school and I was too embarrassed to let him know that no one had asked me from my school. He was not concerned with that at all as long as he could be with me and that is what made me love him even more.

The day finally arrived for the prom and his Auntie was so very kind to chaperone us because we were not old enough to drive yet. We had so much fun that night and I could have not asked for anything better than to spend it with PJ. After the prom, we went back to my house. I remember laying my head on PJ's lap and then I fell asleep. My mother came in from work and she took PJ home, but she seemed upset with me because she thought that I had sex with PJ and I had not. The next morning she took me to see a doctor and I felt so humiliated because I did not want to get undressed in front of this strange man, but I did what I was asked to do. So, after the examination the doctor assured my mother that I was still a virgin.

After we left the doctor's office my mother started telling me how she got pregnant with my brother Donnie at the age of 16 and she did not want the same thing to happen to me because she only wanted the best for me. I promised her that I was not ready for that responsibility and I wanted to finish school and hopefully attend college one day before I decided to have a baby. She smiled and I knew that everything was going to be alright.

I was at home alone one day and a friend of Donnie's came by to get his guitar, so I let him in because he had been in our house before. I should have never let him in, but I felt safe if I knew you. When Donnie came home and went upstairs and saw that his guitar was gone he was furious and came down stairs yelling at me. I don't know if Donnie learned his lesson about taking other people's things, but now he experienced how it felt when someone took something that belonged to him. My mother had to send Donnie back to Ohio to live with her mother because of all the trouble that he got involved

23

in so that he would avoid going to jail in Kansas City at the young age of 16. Despite my mother's efforts to help him, Donnie became a professional thief and hustler as he got older and spent many years in and out of the prison system. Today, he is a different man who works hard for what he wants and helps others to see that they can change their lifestyle too. I am very proud of him and all his accomplishments that he has achieved in his life.

There were just a few weeks left for school and then my mother dropped another bomb on us. She decided that we would be moving back to Ohio. I couldn't believe what she had just told us, and there was no way that I wanted to move anywhere else because I was very happy where we were. My mother had a good job and a nice house and we all had everything that we needed, so it made no sense to me why she wanted to give all that up and move back to Ohio. She explained that she wanted all of her children to be together once again and she really missed her family. I was very upset and I was not prepared to tell PJ that I would be leaving him to move back to Ohio, but I had no choice because we would be leaving within a few weeks. I never saw PJ again until five years later when we were both adults. I will save the details of that reunion in my next book.

The day before we left, my mother invited some of her friends over, but I was too withdrawn and didn't care to invite any of my friends. I felt like my world was falling apart all over again even more so than the first time we left Ohio, because now I had stability and I was older and attached to people that I truly cared about.

The next morning when I woke up and looked outside my window and saw the U haul truck parked in front of the house, I knew it was real. I didn't have to do much accept pack up my clothes and personal items because my brother Len along with my mother's boyfriend, Butter, carried all the furniture and everything else that we had. I had a terrible feeling about moving back and something just did not seem right. I could not understand why my mother wanted to be with a man like Butter, when he was married with a daughter.

I did not know it back then, but he was the reason why we would be moving back to Ohio because he had already convinced my mother to leave Kansas and give up everything just to be with him. I would often dream about the life I wanted to live once I became a grown woman and I knew that I did not want to depend on any man to take care of me. I had witnessed how the women in my family were treated by the men they loved, and I did not understand why they would stay with these men.

Chapter Four
Back To Ohio

Once we arrived back in Ohio things didn't seem to have changed that much. Ironically, the house that we lived in just over three years prior was just a few miles away from the house that we would be moving into.

It was June of 1979 and I was not happy about the living arrangements because I did not have my own bedroom anymore and I was maturing into a young lady and I needed my privacy. I asked my mother where was I going to sleep and she said on the couch for now until we find a bigger place. I felt so humiliated and left out so I asked my mother if I could go and live with my Aunt and Uncle at their house and she let me go, so that I could have my own bedroom and some privacy. They never asked my parents for any help during the time I stayed with them which only lasted a few months. My mother decided that she wanted me to come back and live with her, and I was not happy about that idea at all, so I pleaded with her to let me stay. She was not giving in to my pleas and I did not have a chance of getting my way this time.

After I moved back in with my mother and two older brothers, I spent endless days and nights all by myself eating chicken wings and greasy fries from the restaurant across the street because my mother was never home to cook any decent meals. I survived the best way that I could and on the weekends I would go visit friends and relatives just to get out of that house. I had an older cousin, Curtis, who would take me out to eat and to the movies often and I don't know what I would have done if I did not have such a loving person in my life at that time. Our mothers were cousins who grew up together in the same household, so they were more like sisters.

I was not looking forward to transferring to another high school, but I had no choice and I was fortunate that my two older brothers were already enrolled at John Adams so I never had to catch the bus by myself. The school was near our house and I did adjust to my new class schedule, but after a few months we were hit with some shocking news. The teachers in our entire school district decided to go on strike to negotiate their new contracts. That meant that we would not have school until they reached an agreement, which did not happen for a few months. I could not have been any happier, so I spent my time listening to Michael Jackson's Off The Wall album. I was crazy in love with him and I was sure that I was his number one fan, and I always will be.

By the time we returned to school after the strike ended it was around April of 1980. I had been working a part time job at a buffet style restaurant that had the best food you could ever want to eat. I kept myself busy working and going to school and now I could buy myself some nice clothes and shoes whenever I needed anything which helped me to become more of a responsible young lady.

I remember one late evening when I was getting off work to go home and I missed the last bus. I decided to walk several miles so that I could get a rapid train that would let me off across the street from my house. It was very dark that night and I was a little nervous about walking so far by myself, but I had learned to keep things inside and I did not like asking anyone for help. The next day when I went to work I told my supervisor, whose name was Yvonne, how I got home and she told me to never do that again. From that day forward she would take me home or make sure that another employee could take me home if they lived near my house. I became very close to Yvonne and I asked her if she could help my cousin because he needed a job.

Actually, it was my brother Len who needed a job, and I don't know why I could not have been honest and tell her the truth, but I was afraid that she would not hire him because he was my brother. Len was a very hard worker and we both had jobs and could earn money to support ourselves because my mother was not giving us any money during that time. I worked there for over a year, but I was terminated because another employee threw some food at me and I threw some back, but it hit another employee who was the cook and she reported us. The entire experience taught me a valuable lesson about my behavior at work and how I should always be a responsible person at my place of employment. I did not have any problems finding another job and earning my own money was very important to me. If an opportunity became available, I would speak up to get the job because if I didn't then I might have missed out.

My 10th grade school year had finally ended in July of 1980, and by this time we had to move out of the house where we were living because my mother was not paying her rent to the little old lady who evicted us. We had to move in with my grandmother Lottie who was taking care of my three younger siblings for the last two years before we came back to Ohio. There was not enough room for all of us in her house. I had to share a bedroom with my brother Len, but at least we had somewhere to live. We knew that it would be a challenge living with Lottie, so we did everything that she requested of us just to keep her happy. We all knew that if she was not happy, we would have to deal with some serious consequences.

I noticed that my mother and Lottie did not have a very close relationship like mothers and daughters should have. This may have resulted from my mother being raised by her grandmother while her mother Lottie lived in New York with Rudy, who was the man that she loved. Well, Rudy broke Lottie's heart and she eventually moved back to Ohio to help my parents with her grandchildren. When I was old enough to understand, Lottie told me the entire story of the lifestyle that she lived in New York City and it seemed so exciting to me.

My mother was not living with us during the time that we stayed at Lottie's house, and she kept telling us that she was working on getting us moved into another home in a nice suburb. I wanted to believe her, but it all seemed impossible because she was always with Butter and not spending any time with us.

I remember my brother Len and I coming home from work one evening on a hot summer day in August. My grandmother Lottie was home alone when we arrived. I was preparing to take a shower and get ready for bed, but my mother came to the house that night to speak with Lottie. The next thing I knew my mother was arguing with Lottie because she had threatened to take my mother to court and fight for custody of my three younger siblings. I had seen my mother upset before, but this time she was crying and telling Len and I to get our things because we were leaving with her and I couldn't grab my things fast enough. I followed my mother down the stairs and I looked back and told Len to get his things, but he was confused and shocked and did not move. I hurried out the door and climbed into the back seat of the car, but I was not happy to see that Butter was driving. We sat there for a few minutes and I was ready to go, but Butter started telling my mother that he did not think that it would be a good idea for me to be out that late with them and that they would come back to pick us up tomorrow. I pleaded with my mother not to send me back with Lottie, but she was persuaded by what Butter had said, so my pleading did not change her mind.

I respected my mother and I wanted to do what she asked of me, but it took everything in my body to make me get out of that car and go back up those stairs. I cried as I climbed one step after the next until I reached the top floor and after all that happened I went to my bed and cried myself to sleep. That would be the last night I saw my mother alive.

Chapter Five
Secrets Revealed

The next morning when Len and I got up the house was quiet, so we talked about what had just happened the night before. We were so upset that Lottie would humiliate our mother in front of us because she knew that my mother was going through a really difficult time in her life. I was angry with her because she did not have any sympathy for my mother and continued to put her down.

My father and his youngest brother, Uncle Tommy, came to Lottie's house that same morning and something just did not seem right to me. As soon as I saw my father's face when he got out of his car and came towards me I knew something was terribly wrong. He hugged me first and then told me that my mother was missing. It was a lie and he thought that he could convince me of that when I knew better. My father told Len and I to get our things because he would be taking us down to Nana's house, which was his mother's house.

It seemed to take forever as we rode in the back seat and I remember praying so intensely that she was okay because I didn't want to believe that anything worse could have possibly happened to her. We waited it seemed like for hours to hear the news about what happened to my mother, but I truly believe that my father already knew and he wanted to wait until the entire family was present at Nana's house before they told all of us.

When my father told us that my mother had been killed, I just fell to the floor hugging my little sister while the entire house was crying and leaning on each other for support. My grandmother Lottie was devastated because my mother was her only child. That was and will always be the saddest day of my life and all that was left of her was my memories.

I knew that my mother was using drugs for a while and I never said anything to her about what she was doing because I did not want to upset her in any kind of way. I could tell she was dealing with a lot of problems when we got evicted, but I was embarrassed and I never wanted to talk with anyone else about my feelings so I just kept myself busy and my mind occupied.

Nothing in the world can prepare a person when they suddenly lose their mother. I never imagined something so horrible happening to her when she was still very young at the age of 36. I had lost my best friend and I knew that my life would never be the same without her.

At the beginning of this story I revealed that my grandmother Lottie finally told me the truth concerning the lifestyle that my mother lived. She obviously felt that since I was an adult now, I would be able to handle the bitter truth as to why my mother was murdered so violently. Her death was ruled as a homicide according to the police department. She was shot several times according to the coroner's report.

I tried to picture in my mind what my mother went through during those last seconds as she tried to fight for her life, but she was no match for the hit men who wanted to make sure she was dead. I was so angry that no one was there to protect my mother, especially

Butter because she was always with him and rarely with us and I knew someone must have known something.

I reflect back to the time when I was about 10 years old and my mother and Butter took me on a trip with them to Philadelphia. I was very excited, but none of my other siblings could go. We arrived at a very big house which had about four floors, and I had never seen anything so huge in my entire life. I believe these homes were known as a "brownstone".

When we arrived, an older lady had come outside on the porch and greeted us with a warm and friendly smile. My mother told me that I would be staying there for a little while and I would be taken care of very well. I was a little nervous about her leaving me with strangers because I thought that her and Butter would be staying too since it was our vacation.

After my mother and Butter drove away I felt abandoned, but the little lady did take very good care of me. She was very pleasant to be around and I really enjoyed all the meals that she prepared for me and her son, who was about the same age that I was. She would take us to church with her a few days a week and I did not like all the shouting and jumping around that they did, but I just sat there until it was time to leave. When we arrived back at the house, she would prepare dinner and would always give us dessert after and then we would play games or just sit out on the porch until it was time to go to bed.

I remember so vividly like it was yesterday, when her son had come home from playing outside one afternoon and the police had escorted him back to the house. He was playing basketball with a few of his friends which happened to be near where the trains would go by. The ball bounced over the fence and they all decided to go and try to retrieve the ball, but one of the boys fell on the track and he could not get up because he was caught on the rail. His friends tried to rescue him, but the train was approaching too fast and both of his legs were amputated right there on the track.

The train eventually stopped and the boy was rushed to a nearby hospital for emergency care and he did survive, but her son was in shock and could not even talk about the tragedy that he had just witnessed. I was very upset just hearing about what happened and I really missed my mother and I wanted to go home, but I did not know when they would be returning to pick me up.

Eventually, they made it back and I could not have been any happier to finally go home and be with my brothers and my sister. I was just a little girl and I did not understand what possibly could have happened to me because I was left with strangers and I really had no one there to protect me. Many years have gone by and even though I can't remember any of the people that I met when I was there in Philadelphia, I will never forget the fond memories.

My grandmother Lottie knew about the decision my mother had made to become a drug informant for the FBI. Now, it all began to make sense to me why we were moving from state to state and school to school so that our lives would be protected forever, but that plan failed. The FBI gave my mother a choice of serving at least 20 years in Federal prison or becoming a "snitch" to work with them in their investigation to arrest several drug dealers. They secured a job for my grandmother at General Motors in Ohio so that my mother would not have to worry about her and they also made sure my mother was employed at the same company when we were living in Kansas City. My mother was never to return to Ohio after she agreed to enter into the Federal Witness Program, but she was coerced and deceived by her boyfriend Butter, who left her for dead. He didn't want to take the blame for snitching on the drug dealers. I never trusted him and it became clear to me why I didn't from the first day I met him.

The truth of the matter was Butter took the stand against the drug dealers who murdered my mother. He was a coward and used my mother like she was nothing but a pawn in a chess game. He saw a young and vulnerable young woman with an addiction problem and he enticed her with money, drugs, and material possessions to draw her into a world she wasn't ready for. My mother fell for his charming personality and good looks, but she did not see the harm of being in a relationship with Butter even though he was married during the entire time they were together up until her death.

I never understood the reason why my mother wanted to be with a man like him when she could have been with someone who deserved a beautiful woman like she was. She was caught up in the street lifestyle that so many young women find themselves a part of and when their men get arrested or murdered their fate is always similar. Butter was a drug informant before my mother ever met him and he had several names that he would go by to keep people confused about who he really was and he did whatever he had to in order to use people and manipulate them to his satisfaction. He never loved my mother and he proved that on the night she was murdered. He intentionally left my mother at a bar late in the evening one night and never returned to pick her up. My mother had no choice but to call her best friend Debbie to let her know that she would walk around to her apartment because the bar was closing. There was a nice young man that was present at the bar that night, who offered to walk my mother around to Debbie's house so that she would not be alone walking in the dark. When they arrived at Debbie's apartment the two hit men were waiting for them behind the garage so they never expected anything dangerous happening to them.

Debbie confessed years later that she heard my mother screaming out her name for help while the gunshots were repeatedly being fired right below her window and there was nothing that she could do to change anything, but she knew that my mother was set up by Butter. After the gunshots had stopped Butter told Debbie that they had to leave her apartment right away and when they went outside my mother's body was laying on the ground bleeding and they both walked right past her like they never knew her. I did not see Debbie again until a year after my mother was murdered when she came into the department store where I was working during my last year in high school.

I noticed her walking towards me and it startled me at first and suddenly I felt sick to my stomach. I tried to avoid her by turning around and walking the other way, but I noticed Butter was standing right by the entrance of the store. Debbie called out my name a few times and I stopped and turned around in her face to let her know that I had nothing to say to her and to get away from me. She pleaded with me to hear her out and I walked away and went to my manager's office to let him know that this woman was harassing me. My manager called the police and they came to the store within minutes and told Debbie and Butter that they were never to enter that store again harassing me or they would be arrested.

I never saw Debbie again after that day, but I did see Butter about five years later sitting in a car that I parked next to at a convenient store. I just stared at him from a distance and he never knew that I was looking right at him with disgust and hate. Life does go on and in time I learned to deal with my grief. When my father told me that Butter had died in prison of AIDS just a few years after I saw him, it was a relief for me and all that he put my mother through when she was with him.

Chapter Six
Life Goes On

I was a grown woman when I asked my father why he did not stay with my mother and keep his family together and he told me that my mother chose to be with Butter once he came home from prison and he was not going to stand in the way of her happiness. As I got older I knew that my father was a street hustler, but he treated me like a princess and would buy me anything that I asked for. He would walk me up and down the streets of Cleveland telling me stories of how women who were once beautiful allowed their men to turn them out on drugs which led most of them to prostitution just to take care of their drug habits.

My father wanted me to see the end result of what happens when a woman doesn't use her brain to take care of herself instead of just her body. He did not want me to end up in the same predicament that numerous women found themselves in with no way out except prison or death. I paid attention to every word that he said and it had a profound effect on my life and I will always be grateful to my father for telling me the truth so that I could protect myself at all times and beware of anyone that tried to take advantage of me.

After I graduated from high school I went off to college so that I could become an independent woman and make something of myself and not depend on anyone for anything. I did not want anyone to have control over what I decided to do with my life or my money. My mother would often tell me that I would be an educated and proper young lady one day when I finished college because she never had the chance to experience that kind of opportunity being a mother at such an early age in her life. Her kind and loving words encouraged me to finish whatever I wanted to accomplish in my life and never give up in pursuing my goals and dreams and I promised her that I would.

I wanted a good life and I knew that I had to choose a man that wanted the same things in life that I did, so I set standards for myself. When I was in high school I met a nice young man by the name of Dre who was a member of the basketball team. It was a coincidence meeting him because my friend Dionna kept telling me about this handsome guy that was in one of her classes that I just had to see and it happened to be Dre. We would stand outside of our typing class and wait for Dre to walk by. I don't know if I would have ever noticed him on my own because I was not the kind of young lady who would go looking for guys to date.

I believe that Dionna really liked him, but she would only talk about all the other girls that liked him and she never told me that she had any interest in Dre. One day while we were both in the hallway I decided to speak to him because he would never say one word to me, so I took the chance to speak first. It was an instant attraction that we both felt and that was the beginning of our courtship. We had only known each other for a few months and it was time for Dre to start planning for his senior prom and he asked me to be his date. I had to ask my grandmother Lottie first before I said yes to his invitation, but she did give me her permission to attend the prom with him.

Well, the prom day had finally arrived and I was very excited to get ready and attend the prom with Dre, but he never called me as the time drew near for him to come and pick me up. I called his house several times and his mother kept telling me that he was not home. I was very annoyed by this because he was either coming to get me or he was not coming, but I wanted answers. Dre finally called me back and I wanted to know what was going on with him and why he was not at my house to pick me up. He told me that he had changed his mind about going to the prom because his mother did not get the rental car that he wanted. I let him know that if he did not come and pick me up and take me to the prom that he invited me to attend, I would never talk to him again and I meant that. By the time Dre picked me up and we arrived at the prom, three hours later, it was over and everyone was getting ready to leave. However, we did take a picture and I really didn't even want to do that, but a few of my friends who were there pleaded with me, so I went ahead and took the picture.

We left the prom and Dre took me home to change clothes to attend the after party, but first we stopped at a neighborhood restaurant where they served greasy fries and shrimp for something to eat. We arrived at the party and I refused to dance with Dre the entire night, but I had such a wonderful time dancing with everyone else that I forgot all about the prom. Dre took me home and I told him that I did not want him to ever call me again and he didn't. I knew that he went off to college, but I did not know where.

The next time that I saw him was during my senior year in high school when he attended one of our basketball games and I was on the dance team. I was really shocked at his appearance because he had changed so much physically. He was no longer the skinny kid that I met during his senior year, but he was a muscular and well defined man who had confidence about himself and I was really impressed with that. We briefly spoke to each other in passing, because I was with my boyfriend at that time. However, we did get a chance to talk because he attended the party after my high school prom. He asked me about where I was going to college and at that time I had not decided what university I wanted to attend. He told me about his college and asked me if I would come with him for a visit. I told him that I would have to ask my grandmother because I was still a minor at that time.

After graduation in June I turned 18 years old and made my own decision to visit the campus with Dre. I really liked the campus and I would only be an hour away from home which would allow me to see my family every weekend. It was the best choice that I could make for myself and very convenient because I would have to travel by bus back and forth which was economical and convenient for a college student. I continued to work through the summer and save money because my grandmother Lottie told me that I would be on my own if I decided to move out and attend college. I was eager to be on my own and prepare myself for the college experience. I wanted to return to Kansas for a visit before I started school in the fall.

It had been four long years since the last time that I saw PJ and he was waiting right there when I stepped off the bus and into his arms. We had continued our friendship over the phone and writing each other letters over the years. We were both adults now and mature enough to spend time together without any supervision. I stayed with PJ at his Aunt Debbie's house for an entire month and he was still the kind and gentle young man that I had met when I was 12 years old.

We had so much fun together doing whatever it was that we decided to do and every day that I spent with him was like a dream come true. PJ had his own car and I would go to work with him and help him, but he really didn't need my help. He took me on a trip to Louisiana where we would attend his family reunion and everyone was so nice and welcomed me like I was already a family member. We talked about getting married and having a family one day in the future, but there was only one thing standing in our way, my family.

PJ did not want me to return to Ohio, but I was very young and I could not see myself leaving my little sister who needed me after losing our mother just a few years before. PJ would be attending college in the fall as well and he wanted to take me for a visit to his campus, so that he could get registered for classes and move into his dorm room. We only had a few days left before I had to return home to Ohio and when that day came it was very sad for both of us. I remember getting on that bus and waving goodbye to PJ, and I knew it would not be the last time that we would see each other because we promised to always keep in touch no matter what distance was between us.

My college experience was exciting and challenging all at the same time. You meet new friends and then you lose old friends. There was so much jealousy and back stabbing that went on the entire time that I attended college and it seemed to be no different than being in high school. I was getting frustrated because I did not like the hardships that I had to endure and I had little family support the entire time that I lived there. Dre was very supportive with anything that I needed help with and he even gave me the money so I could move into the dormitory.

I joined an organization for young women who provided support to their fraternity brothers because I wanted to belong to something positive, but only negative situations arose from that. For example, some of the women were sexually assaulted, but was too afraid of telling anyone for fear of embarrassment. There were many fights that took place because guys would cheat on their girlfriends and when the girlfriends found out they wanted to fight the girls they were cheating with. It was terrible to witness all this chaos among young people who were supposed to be educated and striving for a successful future.

I had to experience this on a personal level when a young lady who was a very good friend of Dre's started showing him unwanted affection and would do anything for him that he asked even though she knew we were dating each other. She was so upset and jealous when she found out that I was pregnant with Dre's child. So, she started spreading rumors about me and had even planned to have a group of girls jump on me despite my fragile condition. I was ready with my knife under my sweatshirt for this girl who thought she was going to hurt me or my child. When she came towards me, I pulled out the knife ready to stab her and a guy that also lived in the dorm came between us and took the knife out of my hand. The police were called to the dorm and I explained what had just taken place because she threatened to hurt me knowing that I was pregnant. They told me that I could press charges at the court house, but I declined and just avoided her as much as I could.

Dre took matters into his own hands by slamming the girl who tried to assault me up against a wall and told her that she was never to come near me again and she didn't. I avoided all those girls who were trouble makers and kept to myself up until the time I moved out of the dorm and returned back home preparing for the birth of my child.

Chapter Seven
Parenthood

It was my plan to be married before I had any children, but at the age of 21 years old I became a mother to my first son on August 22, 1985. I was very happy to have this new little boy in my life and I was determined to be the best mother that I could be.

I went back to finish school when he was three weeks old and it was very difficult with a newborn baby, but I refused to make excuses for myself just because I had a new responsibility. My days were busy taking care of him and studying while he was sleep, but I loved every minute of being his mother. I stayed focused on my goal and I finally graduated 18 months later, and now I would be able to start the career I had dreamed of.

I began my career as a court stenographer in the criminal justice system which gave me an idea of what my parents experienced when they were charged with a crime and had to come before a judge to receive their punishment. I was very proud of my accomplishment, but I often felt disappointed about the way people who were charged with a crime were being treated by professionals in the criminal justice system. They may have been indigent and could not afford an attorney to give them the best advice, but they still deserved to be treated fairly. I became sympathetic to these people because they reminded me of the issues that some of my family members were dealing with and maybe if things were different for them, they would not have been in the situation that they were facing.

Dre and I had so much in common being that his parents had drug and alcohol addictions and so did my parents. My father had been in and out of prison during my childhood and his father had been in prison from the time he was a little boy and he never had a chance to live in a household with his father. Our mothers were left raising the children and living with men that did not respect or love them the way that they deserved to be loved. We both knew what it felt like when our parents could not attend our school functions because they were dealing with all kinds of problems.

Children have a natural affection for their parents no matter what is going on in their lives, but they need to be nurtured and cared for by the people who are responsible for bringing them into the world. Growing up in the environment that we did made me want to work even harder not to get involved in anything that would destroy my life or the lives of my children. I was determined not to have a dysfunctional family, and I never gave up hope that it was possible to have a life that I deserved to live and to finally break the cycle of raising children without their father.

Four years later I became pregnant with my second child. Dre had recently lost his job due to a lawsuit and his attorney advised him not to work until the lawsuit was settled, and he decided to sell drugs to make some fast money. I was totally against this because there was no reason for him to become a drug dealer no matter what he was experiencing in his life. I told him that it was stupid and we had a terrible fight about it. He pushed me up against a wall with his hands around my neck and I couldn't breathe until he let go when his sister came to my defense. I called the police and when they arrived I told them that he had drugs in the apartment, but they seemed not to care about that.

They asked me if I had somewhere to go and I told them that I did. I picked my son up and I left and I knew that I could always go to Lottie's house no matter what the situation was. I was very angry about the entire altercation and I could not believe that he would disrespect me by putting his hands on me when he knew that I was a few months pregnant. I made a choice to leave instead of putting my life and the life of my son in jeopardy because he wanted to sell drugs.

I wanted nothing to do with that kind of lifestyle because I knew that it was not going to benefit me or my children. I had to stand up for myself and fight for what was right and I was not willing to change for anything, not even love. I saw something in Dre that I had never seen before and I knew that I would be taking a chance if I stayed with him.

Lottie warned me that if I stayed with a man like Dre my life would be full of grief and violence because she had seen that happen to women many times before. I did not make any excuses for Dre, and I honestly understood what she was telling me, but I wanted my children to grow up with their father.

After we spent a few months apart, Dre had apologized to me for what happened and promised that he would never put his hands on me again. He asked me if I wanted to get married and we took our vows on October 7, 1989 and began our new life as husband and wife.

The years seemed to be passing by so quickly and we were excited when our third son was born in the fall of 1993. I loved being a mother to my sons and I enjoyed helping them with their homework or whatever they needed help with. They were my life and I never put anything or anyone before them. I try not to judge people based on where they live or the cars that they drive because it's not my business. Instead of working hard for what you want, there are people who choose to pursue a street lifestyle so that they can have the finer things in life. What they don't consider is the lengthy prison sentences they will be given when they are arrested and all their material possessions will be seized or confiscated by the authorities. Greed can make a person do unimaginable things and before they realize it they are caught up in the street life which eventually ends with prison or death.

Chapter Eight
Family Ties

My siblings and I had been through some very difficult times throughout our childhood, but we had always remained close. When I found out that my youngest brother Jay got involved in the drug business I was very disappointed in him. He had graduated from high school and even went on to college, so why would he want to go down that wrong road? He was a very intelligent young man who had ambition and could accomplish anything that he put his mind to. I did not want him to become a second generation drug dealer, but that was the reality and no one was going to get in his way.

He bought expensive cars, clothes and jewelry because now he had the money to do so. He was not a selfish person at all and shared his new found wealth with family and friends. I was not oblivious to what he was doing and I could have made the decision not to associate with him because I knew that his lifestyle was dangerous, but he was my little brother and when he came to visit me I had no problem opening my door to him.

When it came to family, I am the one who would open her house up to everyone so that we could get together to share a meal or stay up all night laughing about the good old times growing up as kids. We would go on vacations together and have so much fun, but that all ended abruptly with what happened next.

In 1994 my brother Jay was arrested with 16 other people in a drug conspiracy case in Columbus, Ohio. His wife Tara, her sister and even our grandmother, Lottie, were all indicted on money laundering charges. The Federal government labeled him as a drug "kingpin" and he was facing at least 30 years in prison unless he accepted a plea deal to inform them about his drug affiliations.

In 1995 he decided to accept a 10 year sentence with the provision that his wife, her sister and our grandmother not be charged with any crime or do any time in prison. I was very unhappy when all of this took place and that Jay had to go away from his wife and children for a very long time, but this is the sad reality when you live that kind of lifestyle. I would tell Dre about the dreams I would have of the police coming to our house and knocking down the door, but I didn't understand why I would have those dreams. We were taking care of our children and minding our own business, but somehow my dream was about to become a reality.

I actually thought I was dreaming when I was awakened by a very loud noise that sounded like thunder one early August morning in 1996. By the time I got out of my bed and stepped onto the floor there was a police officer standing right in front of me with a gun pointed directly at my head. I was beyond shocked and scared out of my mind all at the same time. The police officer instructed me to come out of the bedroom right at that very moment, but I told him I had to get my daughter who was only eight months old at the time first. He watched my every move while I picked up my daughter off the bed and walked into the living room.

I realized that this was not a dream anymore, and I had a terrible feeling that something like this would happen one day, but I just did not know when it would happen. It was not the city police

50

who had just entered my home with their search warrant. It was the FBI and I wanted to know what they wanted because I knew they had obviously made a mistake breaking in like we were on the most wanted list. The FBI agents informed me that they were at my home looking for drugs, expensive jewelry and the least of all, money. I assured them that we did not have any of that and if we did have what they were looking for they would have been at my home a long time ago.

They continued with their search while they rummaged through all the cabinets and drawers that they could find. I asked them what all of this was concerning and the chief FBI agent showed me a picture of my husband Dre who they were there to arrest. Suddenly, all of the FBI agents ran out of my house while Dre was pulling up in the driveway, and I jumped off the couch to see what was happening. One of the FBI agents told me to go back and sit down.

It was so confusing for me and my children who were all sleepy at the time because it was very early in the morning and they did not understand what was going on. I asked them what was Dre being arrested for and they could not disclose that information to me. They did ask me if I knew anything, would I help them and I politely told them that I would never help them because they were the reason why my mother was killed. One of the agents wanted to know why I would say something like that and I told him that since they were the FBI then they should go and read their files because they had access to any information that they could possibly want to know about. I knew they were responsible for what happened to my mother, but none of that mattered because I would never have a chance to read about the case when the records were sealed indefinitely.

After the FBI agents were done destroying my home, they told me I would have a tough time cleaning up the mess that they had left. I politely told them that their day would come when they would have a tough time dealing with the unexpected, but I don't think they could process what I had just told them so they finally left.

At that time my father had been living with us after he was released from prison about a year before all of this took place. Ironically, he was not home during the time the FBI invaded our home and he seemed so shocked at what had just taken place when he arrived after everything that just happened. I learned later that my father was communicating with my brother Jay the entire time that he was living at our house and he had only wanted to live with us so that he could give information to Jay. Once Dre was arrested my father moved out of our house shortly after and never said a word to me about anything else concerning Dre's case.

It's unthinkable that the people you trust are the ones who will betray you and they don't seem to care if it destroys the relationship that they have with you. I didn't let the situation get me down at all because I had survived through a lot of difficult problems before, so I had a tough skin. I started to clean up the house one room at a time and it did not take me very long, but I was left with the dilemma of finding an attorney that could get Dre out of jail. I tried calling Dre's best friend Lars, but he was not responding to any of my calls. Imagine how shocked I was later that evening when I saw Lars on the six o'clock news being arrested by the FBI in a drug conspiracy to sell cocaine.

I was in utter disbelief and from my knowledge Lars had started his own contracting business. Whenever I would see him he would have on a painter's jumpsuit that looked as if he had been working all day long without a break on a construction site. Lars was a veteran who served his country and decided to pursue the American dream. I never expected him to be involved in selling drugs which was a big disappointment.

After a few days had passed by, I had to appear at the Federal courthouse because Dre and about ten other people were being arraigned on various federal charges. When Dre entered the courtroom he had his face down and the T-shirt that he was wearing was turned inside out, possibly not to embarrass his fraternity. I couldn't believe that I was going through the exact same situation my mother had experienced when my father went away to prison. I wanted nothing to do with the drug lifestyle no matter how much money was involved, but I was entangled right in the middle of this vicious trap.

I knew that nothing positive would ever come from dealing drugs. I would never condone anyone who chose a lifestyle that would result in nothing but a sad ending. Unfortunately, that is what happened with Lars after the judge sentenced him to life in prison. I was very angry that I had to call relatives and friends for help, but Dre needed an attorney with experience in Federal court cases. I found one and his retainer fee was $500.00 dollars an hour which was more money than I made in an entire day of working.

The attorney we hired was recommended by a friend who had also needed his services in the past. The first thing was to get Dre out on bail which was done within a few hours after he had been arrested. The judge presiding over the case ordered that Dre be put under house supervision which means you are monitored by an ankle device through the local phone company. Once you have been approved for this service, you are responsible for the monthly payments, and you cannot remove the device for any reason or you will be in direct violation of the court order. That was just the beginning of a very long and tiresome ordeal.

One afternoon I received a call from Dre's attorney and he wanted to talk to me privately about the case, so I agreed to meet with him at his law firm. When I arrived he started to explain to me the seriousness of the crime that Dre was being prosecuted for, which was the unlawful use of a telecommunicated act. I had never heard of anything remotely close to what he was talking about, but these were federal charges and I did not have much experience understanding the federal laws, which were much different from state laws.

Basically, he was allegedly charged with conspiring to sell drugs over the telephone with a known drug dealer, but he was never caught selling or buying any drugs from anyone. So, he was left with the ultimatum of telling on his best friend Lars or doing time in federal prison. Dre's attorney wanted me to go home and talk some sense into his head because he was facing at least 18 years in federal prison if he took his chances and went to trial on his case.

Dre felt confident that he would be found not guilty because they had no real evidence that he did nothing wrong. I told Dre that I would not raise our four children alone if he was sentenced to 18 years in prison. He decided to a plea agreement which was the best decision he could have made concerning his life.

Dre had to appear in court before a federal judge approximately four months after the FBI had arrested him. He apologized for his involvement to the judge and she was lenient with him. Nonetheless, you have to be punished no matter what the circumstances involved. The judge sentenced him to serve one year in a federal prison in the state of Kentucky. The day came when I had to take Dre to the courthouse so that he could turn himself in to the authorities. When he got out of the car, he could not even look me in the face to say goodbye.

It was difficult for me to see him go through that entire ordeal, but he realized that I was right about what I had been telling him for years about the people that he associated with. I knew they were no good for him, but he never listened to me until it was too late. I drove home thinking about my life and how much it resembled the life that my mother lived in so many ways.

I was angry that I had married a man who risked his life and the lives of his family just to be around people who had money and were deeply involved with other drug affiliations. I had no time to dwell on something that was done and over with. My main focus would be my children and how I would take care of them by myself. I never had any doubts that I could handle it because they were my motivation to keep going and I had the best teacher, my grandmother Lottie.

Chapter Nine

Daddy's Home

Raising my children alone was going to be a challenge, but I had to do what I had to in order to make money. I worked very long hours every day so that I could take care of my children and make sure that I spent quality time with them doing activities that they enjoyed. My children were everything to me and I could not let them see me give up on myself or them. I worried about them while they were at school and the day care, but I had no other choice because I had to pay the mortgage and the house hold bills so we would not end up homeless.

I learned so much from my grandmother Lottie, and how she managed to take care of six grandchildren by herself. I drew strength from her example which motivated me to be the best mother that I could be no matter what obstacle was in front of me. I made up my mind at a very young age that I was not going to be a woman who had to sell herself cheap to be with men for money or material things. I was determined to get whatever I needed for myself and my children without the hassle and heartache of being with several different men just because they had the means to buy me anything I wanted.

Many women often times put themselves in terrible situations for financial and maybe even emotional support because our nature as women has always been to depend on a man. But, if their men are not available, what can women do for themselves? They can have confidence that they can and will survive through any difficult situation, and if the man you truly love wants to be with you, then he will come across the universe for you.

I had not seen my husband Dre for several months during his time in prison. I decided to take some time off work and drive to Kentucky to visit him. The entire process of visiting an inmate in prison can be exhausting. There are so many rules that the inmate has to follow or else their visits can be terminated.

The boys were very happy to see their father, but our daughter was only two years old at the time and she did not even want him to hold her. I believe that most children have a tendency to forget a person that they don't see on a daily basis because that bond has been broken, which was the case with our daughter. Our visit lasted only a few short hours and then it was time to say goodbye. Dre's pride was crushed after we had left and he told me that he did not want us to come back to visit him again, so I didn't. Time seemed to go by fast because I kept myself busy working and taking care of the children. I was very happy that Dre would be released soon and I could prepare for his homecoming.

When that time came I asked a very close friend of mine to keep my children overnight so that I could drive to Kentucky and pick Dre up the next morning. It took me five long hours to drive there by myself, but listening to music helped pass the time and I finally arrived there safely. I checked into the only motel that was right across the street from the prison. It was very convenient for people who wanted to stay overnight after driving a very long distance without turning around and driving back within the same day. I had a very difficult time trying to fall asleep that night because I was in a strange motel all alone in a place that was not familiar to me and it seemed to be creepy which made it worse, but I managed to get through that night miraculously.

The next morning couldn't have come fast enough for me. After I got dressed, all I had to do was drive across the street to the entrance of the prison and wait for Dre to be released. As he walked out the front doors I ran straight into his arms and it felt really good that he could be reunited with his family again. We were excited to get back home to surprise the children because I had not told them that their father would be coming home. We talked for hours during our drive back home and the time went by very fast. When we pulled up in the driveway the children did not recognize the rental car, but as soon as their father got out of the car they all ran and jumped into his arms. It was a feeling of joy and excitement that a family could be reunited once again, which is the only way it should be.

We stayed up very late into the night talking until all the children fell asleep. I really appreciated that moment because we can often take for granted the precious time that we have with family until they are gone and you can never get that time back. Dre found a new job as a food packager a few days after he was home which was stipulated in his release agreement, but he did whatever he had to for his family. However, after a few weeks had gone by, his probation officer called and informed us that Dre had been released home by mistake and that he should have been sent to a pre-release center first.

I asked her was this really necessary and she told me yes, and if he did not comply there would be consequences. The news was unexpected, but there was nothing that we could do about it. The adjustment was going to be rigorous for Dre because now he had to commute from Akron, Ohio to Cleveland by bus every morning so that he could keep the job that he had just started. He had to be back at the center by a certain time in the evening or else he would have been in violation of the rules. They were not going to make it easy for him to survive, so he had to be vigilant in his efforts to be successful in society once again. Life has a way of teaching us how to cope with problems and I was definitely having my share of them, but I kept my head up and continued to fight for my family!

Chapter Ten
The Set Up

A few years had passed by and we were progressing very well as a family, which was beneficial for all of us. In 2001, we were blessed with another son, and we named him Milan. I couldn't have asked for anything more precious than this beautiful baby boy. There was no greater joy that I could have experienced in life than giving birth to five healthy children with no problems. This made me very happy and grateful because I had always wanted a large family with strong spiritual values and a foundation that would keep my family together with unity.

As a child growing up with both of my parents who never attended church with us was quite confusing for me because it made no sense. I did not like when my parents would send us to our relatives house so that we could be disciplined and told what to do by someone else. I knew back then that I wanted to be an example for my children and raise them with the same values that I wanted to live by. My family was my priority and it was never a burden to take care of their needs. I had always been good at helping others and it was something that I was most proud of.

On occasion, Dre and I would drive our family down to Columbus, Ohio to attend one of my nephew's football games because we were supportive when any of our nieces and nephews participated in extracurricular activities. We would all have a really good time, but I noticed that my brother Jay would never come inside to attend the games with the rest of the family. He would just sit outside the gate in his car until the game was over, and I never thought anything else about it. I have always paid close attention to people and their actions which can tell you so much about them based on their behavior and personality. I found this to be very crucial, so that I would know who I wanted to allow in my personal space and those that I wanted to avoid all together.

In June of 2008, my second oldest son Ree had recently graduated from high school and was offered an opportunity to work as a youth camp counselor during the summer at Ohio State in Columbus and he was very excited to leave home and experience the chance to work with kids. My husband Dre was not comfortable with the idea of Ree staying at my brother Jay's house, and suggested that he stay with a very good friend that he knew in high school who was a school teacher and also lived in Columbus. Ree insisted that he wanted to stay with his uncle Jay so that he could be close to his cousins who were around his age, and we supported his decision because he was 18 years old at that time and was a very mature young man.

Three weeks had gone by and Ree was enjoying working at the camp with the children and seemed so excited meeting new people when we would talk with him. One afternoon while I was at work, I received a call from Dre concerning my brother Jay and Ree. He told me the most disturbing news concerning both of them, and that they had been arrested in Columbus during a drug bust conducted by FBI undercover agents. I was in shock and could not believe what I was hearing on the telephone. I was very angry at the thought of Jay doing anything illegal with my son being present. I was beyond livid and I immediately called my sister in law Tara to ask her what was going on there. When she answered the phone I could tell in her voice that she knew more than what she was telling me about Jay's involvement in selling drugs again.

The FBI released my son that day and Tara picked him up, but they detained Jay along with two other men who were arrested as well. Tara was avoiding my questions when all I wanted to do was talk to my son about what really happened on that awful dreaded day. She had learned how to protect Jay very well and she was evasive when it came to giving up any information when it came to her husband.

When I left the office for the day I could not drive home fast enough. The FBI had kept Ree's phone, so he had used his cousin's phone to call us. I was so happy to finally hear his voice and I wanted to know the truth about what actually happened down there.

Ree told me that Jay had drove to a warehouse to meet a friend and told him to stay in the car, so that is exactly what he did. He was on the phone with a friend when he noticed someone coming towards the car, but he could not see a face because the person had on all black. The next thing he knew someone yelled at him to get out of the car with his hands up and he immediately did what they asked him because they were pointing guns at him. The FBI agent grabbed his arms and threw him on the ground where he stayed face down for at least an hour with his hands cuffed tightly behind his back on one of the hottest days in July.

The FBI agents proceeded to raid the warehouse where my brother Jay, and two other men, who were awaiting the delivery of 300 pounds of marijuana were. They were arrested and detained there until all of them were questioned one at a time. When it was time for Ree to talk with the agents, they took him to another room and asked him questions about what he was during there at the warehouse. He politely told them that he was waiting outside in the car for his uncle. He went on to tell them that he was working at Ohio State for a youth camp and also working with his uncle doing various jobs at a business that his uncle would be opening. After a little time had passed by the agents told him that his story was valid and that he was free to go. But, they warned him to get out of Columbus and never come back there.

Ree was allowed to call his Aunt Tara to pick him up from the warehouse. He could not wait to get out of there and call us to let us know what he had just experienced. When he finally talked with us, he said that he was uncomfortable being at their house and wanted to come home. Dre had told him to finish the summer program at Ohio State and he would drive down to pick him up right after the camp had ended.

Ree really hated the fact that he had to stay in Columbus for another week and be at their house because he felt like a stranger. He said that his Aunt and Uncle started to act cold and distant with him after Jay was released on bond from jail. Ree noticed that Jay couldn't even look him in his face, but he had the audacity to ask him if he told his parents about what happened there in Columbus. Ree told him that he did tell his parents exactly what happened, and he also knew that once he came home he never wanted anything else to do with either one of them again.

A week had gone by quickly, and even though Dre had worked all day he drove to Columbus to pick Ree up. By the time they had arrived back home I was in bed asleep, but as soon as I heard

Ree' voice I jumped out of bed and ran to the door to open it. He came right in and fell to the floor crying tears of joy that he was home. I hugged and kissed him and told him that everything was going to be alright. I was very happy that my son was finally home, but it did not change the fact that Jay was responsible for putting my son through a tumultuous ordeal. What made matters worse to me is how he seemed to be unconcerned about the entire situation and never mentioned anything else about what happened.

It wasn't going to be easy to get over what happened during the summer of 2008, but I tried to remain optimistic about my relationship with Jay after all of this took place. How could he put his nephew in jeopardy when he knew exactly what he was involved in? He was enticed back into the criminal life of drug dealing once again and this time it wasn't going to be a slap on the wrist.

Jay never revealed the seriousness of his case to any of his siblings. He kept his dark secrets hidden very well and never exposed what was really devouring his soul inside. I can't imagine something so heavy burdening me every day of my life with no answers to my problems. Months had passed by and the summer had finally come to an end. The children would be returning to school, and I was always excited to take them shopping for new clothes and supplies. Our family life would be back to the same routine.

I had not talked with my sister in law Tara in quite some time. When she called and asked us if we would attend my nephew's last football game as a senior I was happy to support him and I wanted to be there. Dre was not as enthusiastic about the idea when I asked him if he would like to go. He told me that he did not want to be around my brother Jay after everything that happened while Ree was down in Columbus. I understood his decision not wanting to be anywhere near Jay, but I loved my nephew and I just did not want to make him feel like we did not care about him based on what happened.

I decided to rent a car and drive down to Columbus with my three youngest children in October of 2008 for the weekend. It was very cold sitting outside on the bleachers during the game, but it was well worth it when my nephew's team won. I enjoyed being with my family that weekend and what I remember most is the look in Jay's eyes when he told me that my youngest son Milan looked just like his older brother Nique.

I didn't think anything about it then and I felt that something was bothering Jay, but he never said a word to me about what it was. When I arrived back home Sunday evening, I prepared myself for work the next day and to get back to our family routine. Everyone was doing just fine and I could not have asked for anything more than to have my family together happy and healthy.

Chapter Eleven
Losing Nique

It was a cold November night and I was sleeping comfortably in my bed when I heard some noise coming from the kitchen. It was my oldest son, Nique, who was getting something to drink from the refrigerator. I asked him where was he going in the middle of the night and he told me that a friend of his was waiting for him outside. He knew that his father did not like people coming to the house in the middle of the night, but he was still sleeping and did not hear anything. Nique had asked me to let him out of the front door because it was locked and he did not have a key to the house.

I went to the bedroom to get my keys and I remember telling him that it was not safe for him to be leaving out during that time of the night. He told me that he would be okay and not to worry about him because nothing was going to happen to him. I told him a mother who is concerned about her children will always worry no matter what age they may be. He gave me a hug and left out the door and got into a white SUV truck. I went back to sleep for the rest of the night and got up to go to work the next day. I did not hear from Nique until a few days later when he called my cell phone.

I asked him where was he and he told me that he was in Columbus at his uncle Jay's house. I was shocked and confused as to why he could not have told me he was going there in the first place.

He told me that he wanted to work with his uncle Jay renovating buildings and construction projects. I told him that his father knew plenty of people in Cleveland, and if that is what he wanted to pursue, he did not have to go all the way to Columbus to do that kind of hard work. He assured me that he wanted to move to another city and start a career that he enjoyed doing, so I gave him my full support.

When I told Dre that Nique was in Columbus with Jay he could not believe it. It made no sense because Nique knew exactly what happened when his younger brother Ree was there with Jay back in the summer. We had to accept that Nique was a grown man and there was nothing that we could do if he chose to live there and work for his uncle. We both felt very uncomfortable with his choice to be anywhere around Jay.

When I reflect back to the time when Nique was 12 years old, I noticed how much his attitude and behavior had changed around the time when his father was sent to prison. He began to fall behind in school and get into trouble more often and I would talk to him and encourage him to do better and he promised me that he would. I remember the principal of the junior high school telling Nique that he would end up in prison or dead if he did not stop getting into trouble and hanging with the wrong crowd.

Nique was such a big help to me with the other children and I could depend on him to watch them if I needed to work late or just run errands. I knew that it was a big responsibility for him, but he did not want me to hire a baby sitter to take care of them because he wanted to do it on his own. He would prepare food for them and make sure that they were okay until I made it back home. He was my little man even though he was just a boy.

Nique was happy when his father came home and he started to improve in school with his grades which made us very proud as his parents. He was able to get his first summer job when he turned 14 years old and earn money to buy whatever he wanted.

We wanted all of our children to succeed and do well in school, but a few years later Nique started to show signs that he was struggling again and he could not focus. We transferred him to another school to see if that would make a difference and it did for a little while. Nique wanted to do what all the other kids his age were doing like smoking or wearing his pants low on his hips. His father would constantly talk with him and let him know that it was stupid to be a follower, but he was stubborn and continued to do the same thing over and over again even if it meant that he was going to be disciplined or punished for his behavior.

As a mother I worried about him constantly and I knew that he had challenges that he had to overcome, but it was not going to happen overnight. I had seen all the problems that my mother had to deal with when my brothers were teenagers. I understood and I had compassion for my son and I did not want to give up on him. He would stay out past curfew on several different occasions and the police would bring him home and issue a citation which meant that we had to appear in court.

We decided that it would be best if Nique enrolled in an at risk youth program to possibly help him with all the problems he was facing and take him away from the negative influences of his environment. He was sent to a facility that was an hour away from where we lived, but we went to visit him every Sunday. When we did visit him, he seemed angry with us for sending him away from his family. We were desperate and willing to do whatever we had to in order for him to get the help that he needed.

After six months Nique had completed the program and was allowed to come home with his family. He was in the 10th grade now and looked forward to being in high school. Every day I would drop him off in the morning and go to work right down the street, and shortly after that he would leave school early without permission. He was not interested in school anymore and we were very disappointed when he decided to drop out which hurt us very much.

We encouraged Nique to attend a program that would help him get his GED so that he could support himself. He did attend that school for a little while, but he eventually stopped going.

Nique wanted to stay out all night drinking alcohol and using different drugs. I knew all too well how that kind of behavior affected many of my relatives when I was a little girl growing up especially my own father. He told me how he had abused drugs for many years because I would always ask him how his arms became so scarred which made them appear to have been badly burnt in a fire. I felt very sad that he had to experience such pain due to an addiction to heroin. He could only wear long sleeve shirts so that his arms were never exposed to other people. That image resonates in my mind even to this day and I drew strength from him telling the truth and it made a long lasting impression on me to never have a desire to use any kind of drugs that could lead to a life of substance abuse.

I had an uncle who was a very heavy drinker and you might even say an alcoholic. He would abuse my aunt and call her disrespectful names all the time. I did not like him at all and I never wanted him to touch me when he would ask me for a hug because he always seemed to have this creepy look in his watery eyes.

I was only 10 years old and I remember falling asleep on the couch one night at my Auntie's house. I woke up because my uncle was touching my feet and it appeared that something wet was on my legs, but I had no idea at the time what it was. I jumped up and ran into my cousin's room and climbed into the bed with my brothers and cried myself to sleep.

The next morning I told my two older brothers what had happened and they took matters into their own hands by attacking my uncle. They told him that he better not ever touch me again and after that altercation he never did. I carried the emotional scars around for years and I did not understand it back then, but he did violate my body. I never told anyone else in my family what happened besides my brothers, because I did not want matters to get worse than it already was. I always felt safe with my brothers because they protected me and I could depend on them to help me with any situation. I had confidence that they would take care of the problem no matter how difficult it might have been for them.

I was desperate and I needed help with my son Nique because I knew that he was running around with friends who were a bad influence on him. I asked my younger brother Ty who lives in New Jersey, if Nique could come there to live with him and his family for a while just to get him away from the negative environment that was suffocating him at a very fast pace. I never received an answer from Ty and even though it was not his responsibility to help my son, I felt that it was his obligation as my brother to look out for the best interest of his nephew if he cared about him at all.

Ty had been caught up in the streets as a young teen and knew the struggle of making it out there. He was very fortunate that our grandmother pleaded with the judge, on his behalf, not to send him to a juvenile detention center for punishment. Ty was given an opportunity to attend a program for at risk youths to help them restructure their behavior so that they could become productive adults in society. Ty excelled to the top of his class and he received a full scholarship to play basketball in college. He made some bad decisions along the way, but he did not let his mistakes consume his entire life and prevent him from achieving his goals.

Today, he is a very successful entrepreneur of his own businesses and a role model to children that live in the same community that he lives in. His example proves that you don't have to become an inferior product of a bad environment, and that if you are given a chance to change your life around you can succeed.

Our parents did not leave us a legacy to follow, nor did we have a trust fund to help secure our future in life. We were left to fend for ourselves and make our own decisions whether they were good or bad, but we always seemed to help one another during difficult times no matter what it was. I needed family support more than anything else in my life, but I realized that no one wanted to help us with our son because they were busy trying to raise their own children to be successful adults. I was in a state of despair and I did not want to lose my son, but I was running out of time.

There were nights when I cried myself to sleep because I was fearful of something happening to Nique, and the agony would not let up until I saw him again. When he did come home, he was often high off some type of drug or alcoholic beverage. I would constantly talk to him about what happened to some of my relatives who did those same things and it never turned out good for any of them. I could see the pain in his face, but he was emotionally withdrawn and did not seem to care much about what I was telling him. It was devastating to see my son give up on himself, but I refused to give up on him because I knew that addiction would destroy him if he did not get help soon.

I did not know much about what bipolar disorder was, but my son had all the behavior traits of someone who suffered from this mental disorder. I wanted him to see a physician immediately to see if he could be properly diagnosed. During that time I had learned that my father in law was bipolar and he was on medication to help control his erratic behavior and that this disorder could be inherited through family genes. I scheduled an appointment for Nique to see his family physician so that he could be evaluated to see if he did in fact suffer from bipolar disorder, but unfortunately he never did make it to that appointment.

Nique was using and selling drugs which eventually led to him serving time in prison for about a year. When he was released, we allowed him to come back home if he obeyed our rules. He would try for a while and then his old habits would return. I was very upset to see my son go through the same vicious cycle of degradation and destruction of one's life. I would give him anything that he asked for if only he would accept the help that he needed. I was only his mother and limited in my ability to help him, but there was something in his way and I did not have the power to remove it.

I have four brothers, and three of them have served time in prison at some point in their lives. Currently, I have two nephews and cousins, as well as friends who are also serving time in state or federal prisons today. How can we break this vicious cycle of young men in our society going to prison for committing crimes that are most likely done in their own communities?

The only way, I believe, is to build positive reinforcement in their minds and to educate them while they are very young and help them to understand the knowledge that they can possess before they make the same mistakes that their fathers and grandfathers made before them. They need responsible caring fathers and teachers that really care about them and want to see them succeed in life.

So many of them never even get a glimpse of what that could be like, so they join gangs and give into negative peer pressure to impress people that don't have any more knowledge than they do. The statistics prove that there will be one out of every four young black males who will go to prison or possibly be killed before they reach the age of 25. This is a very sad reality, but one that is prevalent today in the world we live in.

When I found out that my son was in a gang it horrified me because I knew that it was him acting out of frustration and it was a foolish decision. I felt like he wanted to belong to something that made him feel secure and important even if it meant hurting his own family, and we were hurting deeply trying to save his life. We were working parents who provided everything that our children needed, so that they would not go astray and be protected from bad influences. But, as parents we would have never thought that a bad influence could be right in our own family.

Chapter Twelve
News At Eleven

It was a very cold night in December of 2008, and I remember falling asleep for the night. Suddenly, I heard my husband, Dre yell out my name and I jumped out of my bed in a panic. I went into the dining room and when I looked at him he had a look of disgust on his face. He then told me to call my sister in law, Tara, because she had just called his cell phone crying because something had happened to Nique.

I called her right back within a few minutes and she was still crying which made me nervous. I asked her what happened to Nique and she told me that she had seen him on the news, and that he had been arrested involving my brother Jay's drug co-defendant who had been killed earlier that day. I did not want to believe what she had just told me because it did not seem real at that moment. I asked her if Jay was in jail and she told me that he was at home and that she had left him and was staying with her sister.

After hearing all this bad news from Tara I felt sick to my stomach. I laid on my bed trying to process everything that I had just heard in my mind. I never imagined in my worst nightmare that something of this magnitude would happen to one of my children. The next morning I went to work and called the county jail where my son was being held so that we could plan to drive to Columbus and visit him face to face to find out the truth about what really happened and why he was arrested.

A few days later we were able to visit him and I remember clearly the awful smell of the county jail where he was detained. It was the most despicable place that I had ever seen in my life, but I had to see my son and make sure that he was okay. We had to wait at a small window until the correction officer escorted Nique to the booth where he could visit us. He was happy to see us, but when I saw his face I just couldn't take the sight of him being locked behind that steel wall. I started crying so intensely to the point where I could not stand up by myself and I had to get out of that jail.

I was very angry that my son was in jail and now it was time for me to confront my brother Jay. I knew he had to know what happened and I wasn't leaving Columbus until I got the truth from him. We drove to his house, which was about 30 minutes from the county jail located in downtown Columbus, Ohio. When we arrived Jay was not home, and we were not surprised by that because Dre talked about how he knew Jay would not be there and he was exactly right.

Jay had been avoiding all my calls from the time we first learned about my son's arrest. When we arrived at their house, his wife Tara was there with my two nephews and I was not in the mood for playing games. I asked her where was Jay and she was so evasive with the truth. I knew she was lying and tried her best to avoid my questions by telling me that he was busy working at one of the buildings that he owned. I did not want to sit down in that house, and I tried to remain calm because she was at least 6 months pregnant at the time and I knew all too well how a woman feels when she is pregnant.

An entire hour had gone by and Jay had not showed up, which gave me no reason to believe that he would ever arrive while we were there. I was getting annoyed because they were both playing trivial games with my time. I could tell that she was communicating with him through text messages every time she looked at her cell phone and to keep Jay posted up until the time we left so that it was safe for him to return home.

It was getting late and time for us to drive back to Cleveland. Before I left out that house I screamed at Tara and told her to let Jay know that he was a coward and he wasn't man enough to face me about the truth concerning my son. Tara was crying and telling me that she loved me like a sister and would never do anything to hurt my son because she loved my son like he was her own son. I told her that I did not care anything about love at that point, and if my family really loved us, then why would something so terrible like this even happen?

We were tired and angry by the time we left their house and was totally deceived by members of our own family and how their nonchalant attitude came across in such a negative way. It took us two hours to drive home and all I could think about was how I never wanted anything else to do with Tara and Jay for the rest of my life.

It was a Sunday evening, about a week later when we drove to Columbus to visit Nique, which worked out well since we were both off on the weekends. On that very day I remember my daughter saying how it would be a coincidence if we saw my brother and his wife when we got there to visit Nique. Well, it was a coincidence because we pulled right in front of Tara's car and parked. Before I could step one foot on the ground she was right in my face. I politely asked her what was she doing there and she looked as if she had just

76

seen a ghost. She nervously told me that my brother Jay was upstairs visiting my son. I was just appalled at the very thought of him being anywhere near my son.

I could not wait to get inside that building so that I could confront him. When we went to the visitation window we were told by the correction officer that we were not allowed to visit Nique that day. Jay had already signed in to visit him and you were only allowed one visit per visiting day no matter who it was. I pleaded with the correction officer to allow us to visit my son because we were his parents and drove over two hours to visit him. He explained that there was nothing that he could do and those were the rules that everyone had to abide by.

We were very disappointed that day and started to walk out the door. Suddenly, Jay came down the stairs with this wide grin on his face trying to act like he was happy to see us. Dre just turned away and walked out the building and headed back to the car with our daughter and my youngest son. I had waited for this moment for quite a while and I was not going to leave until I talked with him. When I walked outside it was very cold and Jay was sitting in his car. When he got out of the car and walked towards me he had a look of worry on his face. I asked him without hesitation, what happened and why did his co-defendant get killed? He nervously told me that it was a drug deal gone wrong and that Nique was not in any serious trouble at all and he would hire an attorney to help Nique, so I did not have to worry about anything. That was just the beginning of all the lies that he told me just to get me off his back.

Jay had a cousin of ours, by the name of Ray, who called me and gave me a number for an attorney. When I called the attorney he had never even heard of my son, but went on to tell me that he was representing Jay and that it was not possible for him to represent my son as well because it would be a conflict of interest. We decided to hire a criminal lawyer who had years of experience as a trial attorney. He had us sign a contract and we paid the retainer fee to him before he would represent our son.

As time went on the attorney informed us that there would be a bond set for Nique and that he would be able to get out of jail until his trial date was set. We called a bail bondsman and had everything worked out so that Nique could make bail, so our hope was to at least have him home until the trial date was set, but then the unimaginable happened. Nique was charged with aggravated murder and aggravated robbery and his bail was set at one million dollars. The bail was set at such a high amount because most inmates would never be able to come up with that kind of money just to cover the bond, so my son had to stay in jail.

The prosecutor's office had offered my son a plea deal of 18 years to life in prison if he agreed to tell the entire truth about what happened and if my brother Jay was the mastermind behind the crime. I wanted Nique to cooperate with the prosecutor so that he would have a future to look forward to and he was just too young to throw his entire life away and to be the sacrificial lamb for Jay's bad dealings. Nique did not want to cooperate with them and be labeled as a "snitch" for the rest of his life on the streets, so he decided to take his chances by going to trial.

His attorney said that it would be insane to go to trial, and his advice to Nique was to take the plea agreement. The attorney knew that the prosecutor had witnesses and crucial evidence that put my son at the scene of the crime and if he ever wanted to get out of jail he would take the plea deal. Armon was one of the key witnesses, who also happened to be Nique's friend and lived in our neighborhood in Cleveland, but I had never even met this young man.

After four months in the county jail, Armon decided that he wanted a future outside of prison. He decided to tell the prosecutor everything that he knew concerning the case which was videotaped in case he tried to change his story later on once the trial started. When the trial started and it was time for Armon to take the stand and tell his side of the story of what took place he could not even look Nique in the face. He stated that he was invited to come to Columbus by his friend Nique and that they would make some money working for Nique's uncle, but he never knew the uncle's name. Armon went on to say that Nique's uncle took them to a friend of his home, and that they would be doing some work there. He went on to testify that Nique was with him that day, but he did not see who shot the victim because they both ran in different directions when he heard all the gunshots.

There were other witnesses who testified during the trial, but not one of them saw exactly who shot the victim. I was called to the stand by Nique's attorney as a character witness, but it did not help him much at all since I was not present the day all of this happened. The prosecutors were going to do everything that they could possibly do to get a conviction, and so they had to make deals with a few inmates to collaborate a lie against my son. They knew that hearsay testimony was not credible, but somehow they were able to get a few inmates who never even talked with my son, on the stand to help their case in exchange for lighter sentences which no criminal wanted to turn down.

After a long grueling eight day trial, the jury found my son guilty on all charges. We were not present during the verdict which made it easier on me because I did not want to hear any bad news concerning my son. Nique called me at work and told me that they had found him guilty on all charges and I was just devastated and I felt so much pain for him being there all alone with no family support.

I was angry with Nique's attorney because he made a crucial mistake by allowing my son to take the stand in his own defense which was a very stupid thing to do. We were totally against this from the very beginning, but he insisted that Nique testify to prove that he was not afraid and he was willing to tell the truth.

We knew that Nique was not capable of being asked any difficult questions by the prosecuting attorney because of his mental state of mind. When I look back at how the entire trial was handled by Nique's attorney, it appeared that he was helping the prosecutor more than he was helping my son, and it would have made more sense if we would have let the court appointed attorney represent my son instead of wasting thousands of dollars on an attorney who was not willing to fight for my son with courage and dignity. Nonetheless, he went on and took his chances knowing that the outcome was not going to be good.

After Nique was found guilty, the prosecutor offered my son another plea deal of 33 years to life in prison if he was willing to testify against his uncle Jay, and he declined that offer as well. I was so devastated at just the thought of my son being locked away in a prison for that amount of time just because he would not tell on someone else. I pleaded with Nique to just go on and take the time that they were offering him, but again he wanted to show how solid he was and that he was not going out like a "snitch".

My son had to be the fall guy for his uncle, and the detectives knew all of this at the very beginning of their investigation which was deliberately set up by someone, but we never knew exactly who that was. It all made sense to us because when Nique was arrested and questioned by the detectives they had shown him a picture of his father and they told him that he did not look like he was 45 years old which left him confused.

Nique and Armon were released from the county jail, wearing orange jumpsuits, by the detectives after they were questioned on the very same day that they were arrested. The detectives were setting a trap for the person who would unknowingly come to Columbus to pick both Nique and Armon up and then they would have had their third suspect. It proved to us, based on that information, had Dre left Cleveland and drove to Columbus to pick up our son, then he would have been involved in the case without prior knowledge. The only person that could have known about this would have been my brother Jay. I asked myself over and over why he would involve his own nephew in a crime of this magnitude?

Was it to get revenge against Dre because they were in a disagreement about the past? There was no excuse that I would accept from him no matter what it was. I was convinced that my son was set up by my own biological brother just to save himself and his own family. It hurt me to my core that a family member could betray me in this manner. At one time I felt that my siblings and I were very close and that we would be supportive of one another all of our lives, but this ordeal would break me down day by day to the point where I did not know exactly how I was going to survive the outcome.

I never saw Jay again after the last time when we were talking outside the county jail on a very cold Sunday evening. The next time

I heard anything about him was when I saw his face in the newspaper when he was sentenced to eight years in prison for drug possession. There were reporters present in the courtroom on the day of Nique's sentencing and the judge did allow us to speak in his behalf before he announced his sentencing. I apologized to the victim's family for the loss of their loved one because I knew the pain that they felt to lose someone that they loved very much.

I poured my heart out to the judge to give Nique a second chance to become a productive citizen in society because he should not have to carry the weight of what happened on his shoulders alone. On that day all the judge saw was another young black man committing a crime and he gave no mercy to my son even though his attorney pleaded with the judge not to shut the door on him forever and to consider giving him a sentence of 20 years to life, which would have been fair in my opinion.

The judge was more concerned with making an example out of Nique when he sentenced him to life in prison without the possibility of parole. When I heard those words it really did not penetrate in my mind at that time what that meant, but I was just totally stunned and really afraid for my son.

The judge did knowingly state, prior to the beginning of the trial that he knew one of the jurors on the case personally and the prosecutor made sure that the jury was all white with no black jurors selected and that was not by mere coincidence. The judge was more concerned with the trial being a catastrophe that could have been avoided if my son would have told the truth instead of wasting his time and the tax payer's money. The judge allowed media coverage in the courtroom during the sentencing to make sure that his message was sent to anyone who even thought about committing a crime and what the consequences would be if you ever appeared in front of him.

I viewed the judge as being very harsh and prejudice in his reasoning because if this was his son going through the exact same thing, would he want him sentenced to life without parole? I believe that his perspective would have been different if he knew that his son was set up from the very beginning. He would have done everything in his power to help his son no matter what the cost because money would not have been a factor when it came down to helping someone that you love.

I cried as the officers handcuffed my son and walked him out of the courtroom to a cell where he would remain until they transferred him to a facility where he would be detained while waiting on the appeal process which can take many years. Before we left out of the courtroom, the wife of the victim walked over to me and gave me a hug and told me that she was sorry about my son. I never expected that from her and that let me know that she was a forgiving person. She was crying and devastated as much as I was, and even though she did not say it, I knew that she wanted my brother to receive the sentence that the judge gave to my son.

The victim's uncle came up to me and gave me a hug and told me that they will pray for us as well. I understood the pain that they were feeling because I had also experienced the pain of losing my mother that I loved very much. There was no judge or prosecutor who cared enough about my mother to see anyone punished or brought to justice in her behalf which made me even angrier.

I thought that if my son was rich or famous then maybe the outcome would have been different or he might have received a better deal without having to snitch on anyone. I will never know, but what

I do know is that I am determined to help my son and support him in any way that I can for the rest of my life and I know that in time the truth behind this tragic situation will be revealed.

Chapter Thirteen
Surviving It All

As a mother, I have to cope with the pain of losing my son to life in prison for now. However, I am grateful that I am allowed to see him even if it is in a prison visiting room. I personally know women who have lost their sons and daughters to extreme violence that is so prevalent in the world in which we live. Some of those women happen to be my family members.

They have dealt with the tragedy in the best way that they know how. I have to admit that I was angry with everyone that I felt was not supportive of me during this tragic time in my life. There were people that I thought I had a close relationship with who avoided my calls and kept their distance which disappointed me very much. The first thing that came to my mind was that maybe they thought I wanted their money, which was the furthest from the truth. The only thing I wanted was their support and encouragement to keep moving forward.

Their actions showed me that they had no loyalty to me at all and they did me a huge favor by moving out of the way for true friends to embrace and empower me. Before she passed away, my grandmother Nana shared with me the tragedy that she had to overcome during the time when my father was a little boy. She was born and raised in Florida and got married at a very young age to my grandfather who was a very loving and caring man. They did not want to raise their children in the segregated south, so they moved to Ohio for a better life.

My grandfather was an industrious man and worked as a painter in business with his father in law. There was always tension in their relationship and they never worked well with one another, but my grandfather was willing to do whatever he had to in order to support his wife and their eight children. My great-grandfather would give his daughter the money to take care of the family instead of paying my grandfather which was the respectful thing to do since he was the head of his household. Nana said that my grandfather never gave her any indication that he was upset by that arrangement and kept his feelings inside because he was a very proud man.

One day he left for work and he got into an altercation with his father in law and his anger took over. He shot his father in law and his wife, as well as her sister. He had let all the frustration and anger build up over a long period of time and when he exploded there was no stopping him on that dreadful day. He came home and told Nana what he had done and that he wanted to kill her and their children because he did not want to live without them. She calmly told him to sit down so that they could talk about what happened.

The police eventually arrived at their house and my grandmother and all of their children were crying hysterically when they took my grandfather away. My grandfather was convicted of murdering three people and was facing the death penalty. My grandmother pleaded with a panel of three judges to spare his life because they had eight children who needed their father even if that meant visiting him in prison.

86

The priest from the church they attended spoke in my grandfather's behalf on how he was a very devoted husband and father to his children and was present with them every Sunday. My grandfather was sentenced to life in prison, and he never got a chance to see his children grow up because he was killed by another inmate. Nana wanted to share this family story with me because she had lost her husband, father, and other relatives within a short period of time. She told me what helped her to endure was the love she had for her children. She was determined to give them the love and guidance that she knew they would need as they grew into adults.

She also told me that her faith in God helped her persevere during that terrible tragedy in her life and that I would have to rely on my faith and keep a positive mind every day to help me get through this difficult time in my life. She knew that I could do it with prayer which would help me to forgive my brother Jay and accept the fact that my son was a grown man and would have to deal with the consequences of his bad decisions. Of course I did not want to hear that, but I knew it was the truth. I promised Nana that I would do my very best, and that time would eventually heal all my pain and heartache.

Sadly, she passed away at the age of 98, but her legacy lives on with me and the generation to come. I want my grandchildren to understand that family members should support one another and never intentionally deceive or manipulate another person because they are young or vulnerable. It was not by mere coincidence that all of this took place. My brother Jay was caught up in the same malicious life of being an informant like my mother and once you choose that life, there is no turning back.

Once you make a decision of becoming an informant, you must do everything that you are told or you will be forced to serve the remainder of your sentence which could end with many years in prison, or death. The corrupt system we live in will not eradicate drugs being brought into our communities because it generates too much money, and this epidemic does not discriminate based on race. My parents could have possibly succeeded against the odds if it had not been for their addiction to drugs.

The rehabilitation system never worked out well for either one of them because they did not have that positive reinforcement to make their lives better for themselves or their children. I made a promise to myself as a young child growing up around drugs, that I never wanted an addiction that would take control of my life and would prevent me from making rational decisions for myself and my children. I know that my life is a precious gift and I want to use it to help others to benefit by sharing my story of tragedy to triumph and to help motivate and encourage them not to give in to self-degradation.

I want children all over the world to know that it is cool to make good grades and be the intelligent one in their class. They don't have to be a follower, but they can become leaders and choose the right paths in life and have self-respect for themselves. They can become entrepreneurs of their own businesses and break the cycle of business that going to prison brings. I want them to know that you may have many friends before you go to prison, but once you get there, you will see those same friends disappear as time goes by.

My favorite saying is "Love is what Love does", which means, if you really love your family and friends show them in a way that is positive and empowering. Never betray them because you will have to live with the person you are inside and that is a dark and lonely place that no human being would ever want to be.

My mother's memory gives me the courage to continue on this journey and I know that it won't be easy, but I am determined to find a way and I will continue to fight for my son no matter how long it takes.

TO BE CONTINUED...

CPSIA information can be obtained
at www.ICGtesting.com
Printed in the USA
FFOW04n1114290417
35089FF